I LOOKED AGAIN and heard the voices of
many angels who surrounded the throne and
the living creatures and the elders.
They were countless in number,
and they cried out in a loud voice:

*Worthy is the Lamb that was slain
to receive power and riches, wisdom and
strength, honor and glory and blessing.*

Revelation 5.11-12

The Saint Michael Chaplet
A Divine Catechesis on the Angels and Gifts of Heaven

Carol Puschaver

Nihil Obstat:
Rev. Darr Schoenhofen

Imprimatur:
Most Rev. Douglas J. Lucia
Bishop of Syracuse

November 17, 2022

ISBN 9798370427329

*In loving memory of dear ones all
who went home to God in 2022:*

Mary, Margie, Dylan, Elizabeth, Kiley, Elsie, and Ardi

Saints Peter and Paul Catholic Church, Krakow, Poland

Dedication

*To the Most Sacred Heart of Jesus,
with tender, grateful affection.*

TABLE OF CONTENTS

PART I

PART II

PART III

PART I

PREFACE

I first came across a St. Michael Chaplet unexpectedly some years ago when signing in for my usual Eucharistic Adoration Holy Hour. Someone had left behind as a "takeaway" an odd jumble of multi-colored beads in a small heap of disarray. I glanced at the sorry little muddle, puzzled by the broken strand of beads that seemed somewhat similar to the Rosary, except – in place of the crucifix was a medal, a St. Michael medal. Instead of 5 sets of 10 beads for 10 Hail Marys were 9 sets of 3 beads – for what prayer, I was completely baffled. Luckily, knowing of a gentleman who could repair Rosaries, I sent the curious jumble to him. I received it back several weeks later, with word that it was a St. Michael Chaplet. A what?? I soon learned how to pray the Chaplet as part of my getting to know the Archangel St. Michael. Little did I realize the treasure in store. (Puschaver)

The germ of an idea for this small book came to me one Sunday morning before Mass as I prayed the first of the 9 Chaplet salutations:

By the intercession of St. Michael and the celestial choir of Seraphim, may the Lord make us worthy to burn with the fire of perfect charity. Amen.

*Perfect charity ... perfect charity. I turned the words over and over in my mind slowly, as though studying them from every conceivable angle; every dimension. **What does perfect charity look like? What does perfect charity <u>do</u>?** The answer that came to me was the searing image of the Crucified Christ, pouring out His life in the greatest expression of love – of perfect charity – ever known. I went on to reflect on the Chaplet as a whole in the same deliberate manner and came to appreciate it as a treasure*

INTRODUCTION

With the Chaplet that bears his mighty and glorious name, St. Michael, Who-Is-Like-To God, revealed a treasure of catechesis on the celestial choirs of angels and the particular heavenly gifts associated with each. Entrusting this treasure to us, he requested that the Chaplet be prayed so as to honor him and all the angel hosts of heaven, but most especially to give glory to God Who created them and "all things visible and invisible" (The *Nicene Creed*). And with what largesse does heaven respond!

The intercession of angels,
A bounty of heavenly gifts, and
The extraordinary favors promised by St. Michael.

I believe that another gift awaits those who faithfully pray the Chaplet and apply themselves to *"thinking about the things of heaven,"* (Cf. *Colossians 3.2*) and that is a certain sweet awareness of the angels as they go about their day. They have a sense of the presence of these ethereal beings who *"look always on the face of [God] who is in heaven."* (*Matthew 18.10*) And what a blessing this is!

While the Chaplet may be said to consist of five parts[1] the primary focus at hand is the second, namely, the Nine Salutations. It is here that St. Michael introduces each of the nine celestial choirs by name. With a choice word here, an elegant turn of phrase there, and deft language throughout, he creates a wonderfully rich portrayal of the angels. In the way of a master teacher, he engages us, makes us want to "go deeper," and inspires us to reflect, ponder and meditate on these citizens of Paradise. As Prince of the

---

[1] An arbitrary construct created by the author for reference purposes. The five parts, in order, are: Introductory Prayers, the Nine Salutations, the Four Our Fathers, Invocation Prayer to St. Michael, and Closing Prayers.

1

Heavenly Host, St. Michael is a foremost authority on all things angelic. From his singular vantage point, he pulls aside the veil and reveals some of the "inside story," that is, heaven – up close and spiritual.

HISTORY

The St. Michael Chaplet, also known as the Rosary of the Angels, was revealed by the Archangel Michael himself during an apparition in the year 1751 to the Servant of God, Sister Antonia d'Astonac, a Carmelite religious. As noted earlier, St. Michael revealed the Chaplet with the request that it be recited to honor him and all the angel hosts of heaven, and thereby and most especially, give glory to God. The Archangel promised signal graces and favors to all who recite the Chaplet, "**'particularly in such times as the Catholic Church should experience some special trial'.**" (Puschaver, p. 20):

Those who pray the Chaplet before receiving Holy Communion will have an escort of nine angels, one from each of the nine choirs of angels, and

Those who pray the Chaplet daily will enjoy the continual assistance of St. Michael and that of all the holy angels during this life, and

He, St. Michael, will obtain deliverance from purgatory for all who pray the Chaplet and for their relations.

Sadly, the Church was not wanting for "some special trial" when St. Michael revealed the Chaplet during the Pontificate of Pope Benedict XIV (1740 – 1758):

During the 18th century, the Church reached the nadir of its prestige and influence…the decline of the Papacy's vigor[2] the suppression of the Jesuits, the failure to come to terms with the new insights of philosophers [e.g., the Enlightenment, Age of Reason and Scientific Revolution]. These are only some of the manifestations of a general spiritual and intellectual debility.

(Bokenkotter, p. 279)

The St. Michael Chaplet was approved by Blessed Pope Pius IX[3] in 1851, one hundred years after it was revealed to d'Astonac. In witness of the singular favor and regard that the Holy Father accorded to the Chaplet, he granted four indulgences:

I. An indulgence of seven years and seven quarantines[4] every time the Chaplet is prayed.

---

[2] After the death of Pope Clement XII in February, 1740, the Throne of Peter remained vacant for six months until the election of Benedict XIV in August of that year. At the end of the prolonged conclave, the Cardinals finally elected Prospero Lorenzo Lambertini, because among their number he was the least likely to offend "one or other of the great Catholic monarchs [since he] had never traveled outside of Italy and so could not have given offense to any foreign ruler." (Matthews, p. 267)

[3] Three years later, on December 8, 1854, Pope Pius IX proclaimed, *ex-cathedra,* the doctrine of the Immaculate Conception of the Blessed Virgin Mary. (Matthews, p. 281)

[4] As stated in the *Modern Catholic Dictionary*, "as applied to indulgences [a quarantine signified] that the amount of temporal punishment removed [for sins] was equivalent to that remitted by the ancient canonical penalty [a rigorous forty-day

II. An indulgence of 100 days daily to anyone who carries the Chaplet about them or kisses the medal appended to the said Chaplet.

III. A plenary indulgence (complete remission of temporal punishment for sins) once a month for everyone who says daily this Chaplet, on any day when, after Confession and Communion, they shall pray for the exaltation of our Holy Mother the Church and the safety of the Supreme Pontiff.

IV. A plenary indulgence (complete remission of temporal punishment for sin), with the conditions above [on the]:[5]

1.	Feast of the Apparition of St. Michael	(May 8)
2.	Dedication of St. Michael	(September 29)
3.	Feast of St. Gabriel the Archangel	(March 18)
4.	Feast of St. Raphael the Archangel	(October 24)
5	Feast of the Holy Angel Guardians	(October 2)[6]

---

fast] . . . imposed by a confessor . . . The term is no longer applied to indulgences." (Harden, p. 454)

[5] According to *National Catholic Register* staff writer Pronechen, the Chaplet "was approved by Blessed [Pope] Pius in 1851. [He] attached indulgences to it for four different prescribed works . . .these particular indulgences are not now mentioned. In the Holy See's official Enchiridion of Indulgences, Fourth Edition, which is the latest word on different indulgences from in [sic] 1999." (Pronechen)

[6] Due to changes in the Church calendar and liturgical feasts since the granting of the indulgences in 1851, individual feast days for the Archangels, Saints Michael, Gabriel, and Raphael, have been combined into one feast of the Archangels, (with the exception of the Apparition of St. Michael on May 8), celebrated on September 29th. (Puschaver, p. 25)

WORKS CITED

Bokenkotter, Thomas. *A Concise History of the Catholic Church.* Revised Edition, Image Books, Doubleday, 2005.

Hardon, Rev. John A., S.J., *Modern Catholic Dictionary.* Eternal Life, 2008.

Matthews, Rupert. *The Popes: Every Question Answered.* Thunder Bay Press, 2019.

Pronechen, Joseph. *"The Powerful Chaplet Given by the Prince of Angels." National Catholic Register*, 9-29-2019.

Puschaver, Carol. *Though War Be Waged Upon Me: A Saint Michael Treasury of Prayer and Reflection,* 2019.

St. Michael's Fountain, Paris, France

THE CATECHESIS AND POWER
OF THE SAINT MICHAEL CHAPLET

The ineffable richness of the St. Michael Chaplet, coupled with its power as a deeply moving intercessory prayer to the angel hosts, is owing to divine catechist St. Michael, who, as with all he does, undertakes and accomplishes the Chaplet's revelation in perfect accord with the Divine Will. Even as the Rosary of the Angels is taught by the Prince of the Heavenly Host, it is also Divinely inspired, and so, inherently powerful.

Approving the Chaplet as he did in 1851, Pius IX effectively gave his Imprimatur to the divine work. Thus he endorsed and ratified the teaching introduced by St. Michael. This was by no means a small or routine approval. Consider, for example, just some of the scope and import of this Chaplet's catechesis – the ramifications – as St. Michael

> ***acknowledges*** the primacy of God as the source of our help,
> ***underscores*** the reality of an eternal afterlife,
> ***identifies*** himself as "Prince of the Church of Jesus Christ, Chief and Commander of the Heavenly Host, Guardian of souls, Vanquisher of rebel spirits, Servant in the House of the Divine King . . . ,"
> ***affirms*** the existence of good angels and also "rebel spirits," or demons (Let this sink in for a while),
> ***singles out*** from among the good angels, for special recognition and devotion, the Guardian Angels,
> ***mentions*** by proper name only the three archangels referenced in the canonical Scriptures: Michael, Gabriel and Raphael,

introduces the nine celestial choirs of angels, referring to them by the names given in the canonical Scriptures,

observes the ancient hierarchy of these choirs from the highest Seraphim to the lowest Angels, as established centuries before by Dionysius the Areopagite, (a mysterious writer confused with Dionysius in the Acts of the Apostles)

demonstrates the wonderful and instructive complementarity that exists between the angel choirs and the heavenly gifts associated with them,

specifies these gifts, from perfect charity to perseverance in faith and all good works, and *instructs* us as to the gifts and blessings which we do well to seek and strive after,

models and *encourages* intercessory prayer,

reveals something of the blessed communion that exists between the angels and humankind,

upholds Apostolic teaching and ancient Church tradition, and

offers a "rewording" possibility to redress the problematic wording of the Our Father: "lead us not into temptation."

When reflecting on the power of the Chaplet, we find a treasure as we consider those whose help we seek, namely, the Nine Celestial Choirs of Angels. These countless, ineffable angel hosts always remain true to God, conforming perfectly to the will of Him *"for Whom nothing is impossible." (Luke 1.37)* As spiritual, incorporeal beings, the holy angels are not bound by the physical limitations of space and time. Consequently, we implore the help of heavenly beings for whom, **by the grace, granting, and will of Almighty God:**

No whisper is too faint or light too dim.
No thirst or hunger, weariness or disease afflict them.

Neither winter's freeze nor summer's scorch touch them.
There is no mountain too high, ocean too deep,
current too swift, or journey too far.
No language is foreign, no human plan secret,
Nor is treasure hidden or dilemma insurmountable.

(Puschaver, Publication review)

Consider, too, just a small number of ways the angels are lively, marvelously at work in Scripture as they

guard us in all our ways, (*Psalm 91.11*)
minister by countless thousands to the Ancient of Days, (*cf. Daniel 7.9-10*)
prepare Isaiah for his prophetic mission, (*cf. Isaiah 6.6*)
announce the wonder of the Incarnation: *"you will conceive… and bear a Son,"* (*Luke 1.31*)
make the heavens resound with exultant praise: *"Glory to God in the highest,"* (*Luke 2.14*)
comfort Jesus in the Garden, (*cf. Luke 22.43*)
witness to the Resurrection; (*cf. Luke 24.6*)
seal the foreheads of the servants of God (*cf. Revelation 8.3*)

(adapted from Puschaver, Publication review)

And by Divine Providence, they are no less lively, no less engaged among us in our present day and age.

WORK CITED

Puschaver, Carol. Publication review for *Though War be Waged Upon Me: A Saint Michael Treasury of Prayer and Reflection* in **Plot, Line and Sinker,** a blog by Ellen Gable Hrkach, July 9, 2020.

**ALSO REGARDING ANGELS:
ADDITIONAL SOURCES**

Based on centuries-old Judeo-Christian and Catholic traditions that significantly predate the revelation of the St. Michael Chaplet in 1751, our study of angels, or angelology, encompasses a rich and diverse array of sources including:

Sacred Scripture,
Catechesis and commentary of the early Church Fathers, and
Catechism of the Catholic Church.

The Scriptures abound with the presence of angels, as demonstrated earlier. Revered by faithful as divinely inspired, the books of the Old and New Testaments, particularly the 73 books known as the Septuagint, constitute our primary source. Contained within the chapters and verses are the names of all of the nine angel choirs:

Seraphim
Cherubim
Thrones

Dominions /Dominations
Virtues
Powers

Principalities
Archangels
Angels

And the three archangels:

Michael   Gabriel   Raphael

The early Church Fathers comprise the second source. Dating to the first centuries of the infant Church, these luminaries include Saints Ignatius of Antioch, Ambrose of Milan, and the inimitable Augustine of Hippo. The last, of course, is a towering figure who, with his authoritative magnum opus, *City of God*, so greatly influenced the whole of Western Civilization. Augustine expounds on the angel citizens of heaven:

> …as these blessed and immortal spirits, who inhabit celestial dwellings, and rejoice in the communications of their Creator's fullness, firm in his eternity, assured in his truth, holy by his grace. *(Dods, p. 278)*

A second individual among the Early Fathers who warrants our attention as relates to the holy angels is an enigmatic figure whose identity is unknown! This mystery person came to be referred to as Pseudo-Dionysius the Areopagite,[7] a man (or woman?!) long thought to be "Dionysius the Areopagite" found in *Acts of the Apostles*:

> *When [the Athenians at the Areopagus] heard about the resurrection of the dead, some began to scoff, but others said, "We should like to hear you (Paul) on this some other time. And so Paul left them. But some did join him and became believers. Among them were Dionysius, a member of the Court of the Areopagus…" (Acts 17.32-34)*

---

[7] While this figure is commonly known as Pseudo-Dionysius the Areopagite, I will refer to him or her going forward with the abbreviated "Dionysius."

As Luibheid notes, "the [pseudonym] was successful; the spirituality of Dionysius was accepted as authoritative . . . because he was believed to carry authority" *(Luibheid, p. 22)* – so much so that, centuries later, the imposing medieval theologian St. Thomas Aquinas would "quote him about 1700 times." *(Luibheid, p. 21)*

This authority of Dionysius extended to his remarkably influential work, *De Coelesti Hierarchia*, that is, *The Celestial Hierarchy*. It is here that we find both an explication of the hierarchy of angels according to "three threefold groups" *(Luibheid, p. 160),* with the Seraphim being paramount, and an elaborative commentary on each of the nine angel choirs. Brief excerpts from Dionysius are included in the following meditations on the Chaplet salutations to serve as a touchstone and point of reference.

Lastly, published in 1992, thirty years after the opening of the Second Vatican Council and during the Pontificate of St. John Paul II, the *Catechism of the Catholic Church* affirms the "existence of angels [as] a truth of faith" *(CCC 328).* Among the many tenets of this faith are the beliefs that

"Christ is the center of the angelic world,"
Angels are incorporeal beings created by God and endowed by Him with free will,
The nature of an angel is "spirit;" the office is "messenger" (borrowing from St. Augustine),
Angels "have been present since creation and throughout the history of salvation,"
"The whole life of the Church benefits from the mysterious and powerful help of angels," and "from its beginning until death, human life is surrounded by [the] watchful care and **intercession**" of the angels. *(CCC 328-336)* Emphasis added.

The teaching of an Archangel conforms to the teaching of the Church, and the largesse of heaven follows upon the intercession of angels.

WORKS CITED

Catechism of the Catholic Church. Image, an imprint of Crown Publishing Corp, a Division of Random House, 1995.

Dods, Marcus, D.D., translator. *The City of God.* By Saint Augustine of Hippo. Hendrickson Publishers, 2009.

Luibheid, Colm, translator. *Pseudo-Dionysius: The Complete Works.* By Pseudo-Dionysius. Paulist Press, 1987.

THE SAINT MICHAEL CHAPLET

+In the Name of the Father, and the Son and the Holy Spirit. Amen.

O God, come to mine assistance. Lord, make haste to help me.

AN ACT OF CONTRITION

Oh my God, I am sorry for my sins with all my heart. In choosing to do wrong and failing to do good, I have sinned against You Whom I should love above all things. I firmly intend, with Your help, to make amends, to sin no more, and to avoid whatever might cause me to sin. Our Lord and Savior Jesus Christ suffered and died for my sins. In His Name, my God, have mercy. Amen.

Glory be to the Father, and to the Son, and to the Holy Spirit, as it was in the beginning, is now, and ever shall be, world without end. Amen.

THE NINE SALUTATIONS
(Pray one Our Father and three Hail Marys after
each of the following nine salutations
in honor of the nine Choirs of Angels.)

1. **By the intercession of St. Michael** and the celestial Choir of **SERAPHIM** may the Lord make us worthy to burn with the fire of perfect charity. Amen.

2. **By the intercession of St. Michael** and the celestial Choir of **CHERUBIM** may the Lord vouchsafe to grant us the grace to leave the ways of wickedness to run in the paths of Christian perfection. Amen.

3. **By the intercession of St. Michael** and the celestial Choir of **THRONES** may the Lord infuse into our hearts a true and sincere spirit of humility. Amen.

4. **By the intercession of St. Michael** and the celestial Choir of **DOMINIONS** may the Lord give us grace to govern our senses and subdue our unruly passions. Amen.

5. **By the intercession of St. Michael** and the celestial Choir of **VIRTUES** may the Lord preserve us from evil and suffer us not to fall into temptation. Amen.

6. **By the intercession of St. Michael** and the celestial Choir of **POWERS** may the Lord protect our souls against the snares and temptations of the devil. Amen.

7. **By the intercession of St. Michael** and the celestial Choir of **PRINCIPALITIES** may God fill our souls with a true spirit of obedience. Amen.

8. **By the intercession of St. Michael** and the celestial Choir of **ARCHANGELS** may the Lord give us perseverance in faith and in all good works in order that we gain the glory of Paradise. Amen.

9. **By the intercession of St. Michael** and the celestial Choir of **ANGELS** may the Lord grant us to be protected by them in this mortal life and conducted hereafter to eternal glory. Amen.

THE FOUR OUR FATHERS
Pray one Our Father in honor of each of the Archangels:
Saint Michael, Saint Gabriel, and Saint Raphael
and also your Guardian Angel.

AN INVOCATION PRAYER TO ST. MICHAEL

O glorious Prince St. Michael, chief and commander of the Heavenly Host, guardian of souls, vanquisher of rebel spirits, servant in the house of the Divine King and our most admirable conductor, you who shine with excellence and superhuman virtue, vouchsafe to deliver us from all evil, who turn to you with confidence and enable us by your gracious protection to serve God more and more faithfully every day. Amen.

V.) Pray for us, O glorious St. Michael, Prince of the Church of Jesus Christ,
R.) That we may be made worthy of His promises.

CLOSING CHAPLET PRAYER

Almighty and Everlasting God, Who, by a prodigy of goodness and a merciful desire for the salvation of all people, have appointed the most glorious Archangel St. Michael as Prince of Your Church, make us worthy, we implore You, to be delivered by his powerful protection from all our enemies, that none of them may harass us, especially at the hour of our death, but that we may be conducted by him into the august majesty of Your Divine Presence. This we beg through the infinite merits of Jesus Christ Our Lord. Amen.

END

PART II

Cologne Cathedral, Germany

MEDITATIONS ON THE ANGELIC SALUTATIONS
OF THE SAINT MICHAEL CHAPLET

The SERAPHIM

By the intercession of St. Michael and the celestial choir of Seraphim, may the Lord make us worthy to burn with the fire of perfect charity. Amen.

Most fittingly, the first Chaplet salutation is addressed to St. Michael and the highest of the celestial choirs, the Seraphim. True to their glorious name, these are the mighty burning ones, aflame with unfathomable ardor and all-consuming love for God, to Whom, of all the angel choirs of heaven, they are the closest. These glorious beings sing without end the *Trisagion*, or *Sanctus,* the ethereal words of praise to the Most High: *Holy, Holy, Holy,* is the Lord of hosts . . . " (*Isaiah, 6.3)*

Concerning this most exalted of all the angel choirs, Dionysius writes

… the holy name "seraphim" means "fire-makers," that is to say, "carriers of warmth" . . . these names indicate their similarity to what God is . . . the designation Seraphim really teaches this – a perennial circling around divine things, penetrating warmth . . . . It means also the power to purify by means of the lightning flash and the flame. It means the ability to hold unveiled and undiminished both the light they have and the illumination they give out. It means the capacity to push aside and to do away with every obscuring shadow. *(Luibheid, pgs. 161-162)*

By the most efficacious intercession of the Seraphim, we ask a threefold gift:

> To be made worthy
> To burn (with)
> The fire of perfect charity

How deeply meaningful are these lines! We do not ask for perfect charity itself. Nor do we petition outright for the seraphic gift of such mystical burning, as though such entreaty were somehow inappropriate and overbold. Rather, mindful of our faults and failings, we ask, simply and humbly, to be made worthy, trusting that God will take care of the rest.

The beloved Old Testament prophet Isaiah comes to mind for his stunning vision of the *"Lord seated on a high and lofty throne"* (*Isaiah 6.4*) with the six-winged seraphim *"stationed above."* Isaiah instinctively cries out in terror, as a *"man of unclean lips [whose] eyes have seen the King, the LORD of hosts."* In response, he receives a marvel of divine healing and transformation:

> *Then one of the seraphim flew to me, holding an ember which he had taken with tongs from the altar. He touched my mouth with it. 'See,' he said, 'now that this has touched your lips, your wickedness is removed, your sin is purged.'* (*Isaiah 6.6-7*)

I ask myself what perfect charity looks like, and, always, I am drawn to the searing image of Christ on the Cross. Here, the Incarnate Love and Word of the God we cannot see, graphically demonstrated this supreme charity as He offered Himself without reserve for us *"while we were still sinners."* (*Romans 5.8*) Here was the perfect Burnt Offering, surpassing all others, making our peace with God.

Burning

Even as the mystical holocaust of our Savior took place on the wood and altar of the Cross, utterly consuming His Sacred Heart with the flames of Divine Love, so did a counterpart physical "fire" rage violently within and throughout His Body. Scarcely raised upon the cross, victims of Roman crucifixion quickly developed high fever in response to their cumulative grievous tortures. The eminent anatomist, physician, and surgeon Pierre Barbet, M.D. who studied the Passion and Death of Jesus in exhaustive detail, explains

> [the victim's] face reddens and then goes a violet color; a **profuse sweat** flows from his face and from the whole surface of the body (Emphasis added). *(Barbet, p. 82)*

Both the mystical and physical qualities of Our Lord's Passion-fire were powerfully manifest in the person of the beloved stigmatic priest of the 20th century, St. Pio of Pietrelcina, affectionately known simply as Padre Pio. The humble Capuchin of San Giovanni Rotondo, who bore the stigmata most of his adult life, "suffered periods of high fever . . . so high that the mercury shot out of the thermometer" with temperatures spiking nearly to 125 degrees Fahrenheit (51.7 degrees Celcius). The seraphic priest wrote that he was "all aflame . . . consumed by love for God and love for my neighbor." (*Kalvelage, pgs. 21-22*).

Saint John, the Beloved Disciple, so sublimely privileged to rest against Jesus' chest at the Last Supper, (*cf. John 12.25*) tells us plainly, forthrightly, that "*God is love . . . and whoever remains in love remains in God and God in him.*" (*1 John 4.16*) To the degree that charity and love both convey the same supreme theological virtue, perhaps we are asking to be made worthy to burn with the fire of perfect *love*, that is, the love which is God.

Perhaps, with this first salutation, we are asking to be made worthy. . . ultimately . . . of God.

WORKS CITED

Barbet, Pierre, MD. *A Doctor at Calvary: The Passion of Our Lord Jesus Christ as Described by a Surgeon.* Trans. by the Earl of Wicklow. Image Books, A Division of Doubleday, 1963.

Kalvelage, Brother Francis Mary, F.I., Editor. *Padre Pio: The Wonder Worker.* Franciscan Friars of the Immaculate, 2009.

Luibheid, Colm, translator. *Pseudo-Dionysius: The Complete Works.* By Pseudo-Dionysisus. Paulist Press, 1987.

The CHERUBIM

By the intercession *of St. Michael and the Celestial Choir of Cherubim, may the Lord vouchsafe to grant us the grace to leave the ways of wickedness to run in the paths of Christian perfection. Amen.*

With the second salutation, we invoke the particular intercession of the Cherubim, the angel choir second only to the Seraphim. Sacred Scripture introduces these wondrous beings in diverse ways, from "protective spirits and custodians of sacred things" (*Parente, p. 80*) to the "throne-bearers of Almighty God." (Ibid.) Small wonder then that the first angel we first encounter in Scripture, in the book of Genesis, is a member of this choir which guards the threshold of Eden and the sacrosanct Tree of Life. (*Cf. Genesis, 3.3-23 ff*)

According to Dionysius, the name Cherubim: (plural of "cherub")

> signifies the power to know and to see God, to receive the greatest gifts of his light, to contemplate the divine splendor in primordial Power, to be filled with the gifts that bring wisdom . . . *(Luibheid, p. 162)*

As with the Seraphim, we appeal to the Cherubim for another of heaven's precious threefold gifts:

Grace
To leave the ways of wickedness
To run in the paths of Christian perfection.

Once more, we do not pray in a direct manner – in this case to run in the paths of Christian perfection – but rather, first and foremost, for the gift of grace. The petition for grace to be able to run the distance of our life's journey along such paths is telling. It is grace that St. Michael emphasizes first. Not strength or stamina; not direction or even perseverance, but grace – the indwelling of God's spirit and life within our being. Grace is our point of departure.   And our destination.

Far from any mean or passing goal, leaving the ways of wickedness presents a life-long challenge, and we do well to ask the help of angels. The plural of "ways" points to the seemingly endless courses of evil that lure us. Yet, no matter their appeal, and no matter the time, effort, and resources we may have spent in their thrall, we implore the grace to break away, much like the Prodigal Son: *"I shall get up and go to my father and I shall say to him, 'Father, I have sinned against heaven and against you'."* (*Luke 15.18*)

Nor do we leave wickedness only to fall idle or roam aimlessly, without direction or purpose. Rather, by the grace of God, we find ourselves at the threshold of *metanoia,* a thoroughgoing change of self. With this conversion of our entire being, we fix our gaze on Eternity with God. We do not look back, dwell on our missteps, or cling to the past. By and with Divine Grace, we are free not merely to walk, but to run, *"like a hero joyfully runs [his] course."* (*Psalm 19.6*)

You will show me the path of life. (*Psalm 16.11*)

Just as the ways of wickedness seem numberless and beyond counting, so too the paths of perfection. However, several remarkable differences call our attention. The word "path" evokes the familiar image of a recognizable trail established over time and carefully maintained by all who have shared a common journey over the years. Unlike the ways of the wicked that vanish, and *"like smoke . . . disappear,"* *(Psalm 37.20)* the paths leading to Christian perfection have a staying power and a permanence. We add ours to the footsteps of all who have gone before, determined to reach the end goal, no matter the uncertainties, setbacks, and challenges that lie ahead. Forswearing the ways of wickedness, we turn as part of the miracle of *metanoia* to fix our gaze on the dwelling and the glory of God, "Who is our Home." *(Perkins, p. 281)*

Among the Chaplet's salutations to the nine choirs of angels, those addressed to the Seraphim and Cherubim alone reference "perfection." From these most exalted choirs, closest of all the angels to God, we humbly implore gifts of heavenly perfection. May we always have the utmost reverence for these spiritual beings who dwell eternally in the presence of God.

WORKS CITED

Luibheid

Perkins, David, Editor. *English Romantic Writers*. Harcourt, Brace, Jovanovich, 1967. See *Ode: Intimations of Immortality from Recollections of Early Childhood*, Stanza V, line 65, by William Wordsworth.

The THRONES

By the intercession *of St. Michael and the celestial choir of Thrones, may the Lord infuse into our hearts a true and sincere spirit of humility. Amen.*

The Thrones comprise the third angel choir of heaven. Scripture is virtually silent about them, stating only the choir name, the first in a series of the choirs referenced in St. Paul's letter to the Colossians:

> *[Christ] is the image of the invisible God . . .in him were created all things in the heaven and on earth, the visible and the invisible, whether thrones or dominions or principalities or powers . . . (Colossians 1.15-16)*

Dionysius infers from

> [the] title of this most sublime and exalted [choir] . . . that in them there is a transcendence over every earthly defect, as shown by their upward bearing toward the ultimate heights, that they are forever separated from what is inferior, that they are completely intent upon remaining always and forever in the presence of him who is truly the most high, that, free of all passions and material concern, they are utterly available to receive the divine visitation....
>
> *(Luibheid, p. 162)*

Yet, the Chaplet salutation we address to the Thrones at the direction of St. Michael points to a markedly different nature, for by the aid of this choir, we ask that

The Lord [may] infuse into our hearts a
True and sincere spirit of *humility*. (Emphasis added)

It is no lofty or grand bearing that St. Michael attributes to the Thrones, but rather, humility – true, sincere, *divine*. That we might wonder at this seeming discrepancy between an exalted, regal-sounding title and a petition for humility offers a small, yet poignant, and instructive commentary on our fallen human nature. We have only to consider, for example, God's solemn pronouncement in the book of Isaiah:

My thoughts are not your thoughts,
Nor are your ways My ways. *(Isaiah 55. 8-7)*

God gives us a model in the Person of Jesus, Who *emptied himself, taking the form of a slave . . . he humbled himself, becoming obedient unto death, even death on a cross.* *(Philippians 2.7-8)* This same Jesus mercifully anticipates the prayer and yearning of all humankind as He calls to us across the centuries:

Learn from me, for I am meek and humble of
heart; and you will find rest for yourselves.
(Matthew 11.29)

The Son of God, Who washed the feet of His disciples and embraced the Cross, beckons us to learn from and imitate Him, not because He is all-knowing or all-powerful, but because – He is meek and humble of heart.

Qualifying Christ-like humility as true and sincere, St. Michael carefully distinguishes it from its base counterfeit, the false humility that leads to toxic self-deprecation. We belittle ourselves and deny the store of God-given talents and abilities lavished upon us to grow in love for God and neighbor, and build the Kingdom of Heaven among all people here and now. Perhaps more fundamentally, this imposter humility is also an assault upon the belief that we are *"fearfully and wonderfully made" (Psalm 139.14)* in the image and likeness of God, for Whom all things are possible.

The salutation to the Thrones turns on the action word, or verb, *infuse.* Exquisitely rich in meaning, it offers valuable insight into the mystical transformation of hearts made possible by heaven's munificent divine gift of true and sincere humility.

The *American Heritage Dictionary, Second College Edition,* lists four definitions for *infuse*:

To put into; introduce
To cause to pervade; imbue
To give an animating or motivating impulse to
To steep or soak without boiling. *(Berube, p.661)*

The meaning of *infuse*, and by extension, the salutation to the Thrones as well, is all the richer when we consider also two related words, or cognates: *fuse* and *fusion*. This word trio derives from the common Latin root word, *fundo*, *fundere*, a verb having two literal definitions:

As relates to liquids: to pour, pour out
As relates to metals: to melt, cast. *(Simpson, p. 259)*

True and sincere humility infused into hearts is a most efficacious remedy for the deadly sin of pride, the first sin that incessantly trumpets the ancient, deadly lie: *"I shall be like the Most High!" (Isaiah 14.14).* As with a healing balm, humility imbues our hearts, strengthens and disposes them to love the God Who exhorts all people, *"Harden not your hearts."* (*Hebrews* 3.15). It is with true and sincere humility that we live the first and greatest commandment to *"love the Lord [our] God with all our minds, our strength. . . [and the second] which is like it"* (*cf. Matthew 22.37)* to love our neighbor as ourselves.

As noted previously, *fuse* and *fusion* share a common Latin root word meaning "to melt." Small wonder, then, that this nuance of meaning should also lend some insight into the miracle of the transformation of our hearts. Consider the marvel of nuclear fusion at work in our sun, as hydrogen atoms are seared – *fused* – together in such manner, at such extremely high temperatures as to produce a new element of helium. And there follows one of nature's most refulgent, powerful "outward signs" – an explosion of light and heat that makes the far and vast reaches of space resplendent; and the miracle of life on earth possible.

The life-giving cosmic wonder of fusion moves us to consider one further meaning of *fuse,* that is, to "give an animating or motivating impulse to." A fuse is lit – and the brilliant spark, breathtaking vibrancy; the unleashed and urgent force thus generated, all point to the miracle of

PENTECOST!

And suddenly there came from the sky a noise like a strong driving wind ... There appeared to them [the Apostles] tongues as of fire which parted and came to rest on each one of them. And they were all filled with the Holy Spirit, and they began to make bold proclamation as the Spirit prompted them. (cf. Acts 2.2-4)

Mystically fused into every cell of the human heart, with all its frailty and weakness, the humility for which we pray creates a new heart "burning with the fire of perfect charity." If we, like the

Emmaus-bound disciples, should ever question *"were not our hearts burning with love,"* (*Luke 24:32*) may we always be ready to answer with a resounding, wholehearted YES!

YES! OUR HEARTS WERE — AND ARE — BURNING WITH LOVE

At every minute of every day, with every beat, may our hearts pulse with love, because, by the grace of God, and with the aid of angels, they have been joined – *fused* – in communion with the Heart of Jesus, Who is meek and humble.

WORKS CITED

Berube, Margery S., Director of Editorial Operations. *The American Heritage Dictionary: Second College Edition.* Houghton Mifflin, 1982.

Luibheid.

Parente, Pascal P., Rev. *The Angels in Catholic Teaching and Tradition.* TAN Books, 2013.

Simpson, D.P., Revisor and Editor. *Cassell's New Latin Dictionary, Latin/ English; English/Latin.* Funk and Wagnall's, 1968.

The DOMINIONS/DOMINATIONS

By the intercession of St. Michael and the celestial choir of Dominions, may the Lord grant us the grace to govern our senses and subdue our unruly passions. Amen.

Continuing with the celestial hierarchy of angels in descending order, the fourth angel choir is that of the Dominions, also known as Dominations.

Scripture refers to the Dominions two times only – both in the letters of St. Paul. As we have already seen in the letter to the Colossians, the name of this choir is included in a series of four categories of angels. The other mention of the Dominions is found in the Apostle's letter to the Ephesians:

> *Christ is above all principality and power and virtue and dominion.*   *(Ephesians 1:21)*

Whereas St. Paul offers no commentary or detail on any of the above-named choirs – perhaps to emphasize all the more the universal supremacy of Christ – Dionysius associates with the Dominions:

> ...a lifting up which is free, unfettered by earthly tendencies, and uninclined toward any of those tyrannical dissimilarities which characterize a harsh dominion . . . it is above any abject creation of slaves, and, innocent of any dissimilarity, it is forever striving mightily dominion.
>
> *(Luibheid, p. 167)*

The Chaplet salutation to the Dominions corresponds beautifully with this characterization as we pray for another of heaven's threefold gifts:

Grace
To govern our senses [and to]
Subdue our unruly passions

The language of this fervent address takes us back in time and place . . . before the Fall in the Garden of Eden. With a singular benediction, God enjoins our First Parents:

> *Fill the earth and subdue it. Have dominion over the fish of the sea, the birds of the air and all the living things that crawl on the earth.*   *(Genesis 1.28)*

Yet, how very soon after these blessed words of commissioning did Adam and Eve heed the serpent instead:

> *. . . when you eat of the [Tree of the Knowledge of Good and Evil] your eyes will be opened and you will be like gods.*   *(Genesis 3:5)*

Thus the Archfiend seduces Adam and Eve with another iteration of his primeval lie:

> *"I shall be like the Most High!"*

Thus tempted by Satan and enticed by the fruit of the Forbidden Tree as most fair to behold, succulent to taste and desirable for gaining divine knowledge, Eve succumbed, and so:

> Earth felt the wound, and Nature from her seat
> Sighing through all her Works gave signs of woe
> That all was lost.   *(Hughes, p. 396)*

Who could possibly tell of the enormity, the rampaging torrent of evil that so quickly fell upon humanity?! How very soon after the First Transgression do we hear God admonish Cain for the murderous rage and dejection he feels on account of his brother Abel:

> *. . . sin lies in wait at the door; its urge is for you,*
> *yet you can rule over it. (Genesis 4.7)*

One might well contend that in grave consequence of our fall from grace, it was no longer earth's plant and animal kingdoms which had need of our careful dominion. Tragically, that distinction – the need to be governed – now belonged to us.

So incomparably essential to our shared humanity, our senses and passions number among the most highly cherished of God's many gifts to us. With them, are we able to apprehend and engage with the infinite wonders of creation, from the dreamy spectacle of fireflies dancing in the night, to the cool *swoosh* of a basketball clean through the net, to the tangy sweetness of fresh lemon meringue. It is passion, grit and steely determination that carry the long-distance runner to the finish line, righteous anger that will not brook social injustice; and self-sacrificing love and patience that make possible numberless days and years tending to a spouse in the grip of chronic, debilitating illness. Indeed, by such as these and countless other examples, we build community with one another. And, by far, the pinnacle of such exchange is an intimate relationship with our God, as the Beloved Disciple writes with surpassing eloquence:

> *What was from the beginning,*
> *what we have heard*
> *what we have seen with our eyes*
> *what we looked upon*
> *and touched with our hands*
> *concerns the Word of life . . . (1 John 1.1)*

What befalls this sublime communion, however, when our senses and passion go awry? The Apostle Paul gives a blunt and unsparing answer:

> *... the flesh has desires against the Spirit ... [and] the works of the flesh are obvious: immorality, impurity, licentiousness,   idolatry,   sorcery,   hatreds,   rivalries, jealousy, outbursts of fury, acts of selfishness, dissensions, factions, occasions of envy . . . . (Galatians 5:17,19-21)*

Paul is still more to the point in his letter to the Romans:

> *The wages of sin is death.   (Romans 6.23)*

But thanks be to God, (*1 Corinthians 1:57*) death is far from the last word, even as the Apostle goes on to proclaim with a flourish of triumph:

> *The gift of God is eternal life in Christ Jesus our Lord.*
> *(Romans 6.23)*

And again:

> *Death is swallowed up in victory.*
> *Where, O death, is your victory?*
> *Where, O death, is your sting?*
> *But thanks be to God who gives us the victory*
> *through our Lord Jesus Christ.*
> *(1 Corinthians 1:54,55,57)*

In the never-ending and oft-supremely daunting challenge of mastering our wayward senses and passions, the Dominions, among all the angel choirs, appear to have the special charge of aiding us. They stand out as the "go-to angels" when these so integral and inextricably joined dimensions of our human nature would transgress the boundaries of moderation, temperance, and self-discipline essential for living the two Great Commandments.

Let us grow in mindfulness of the Dominions and turn to them often as we strive to –

> resist temptation and the false glamor of evil,
> conquer habitual sin, and
> avoid the "near occasion" of sin.

With the unfailing strength, support and encouragement of these blessed angels, may we lead authentic Christ-centered lives and do all to the best of our ability for the greater honor and glory of God, and good of neighbor.

And by all means, remember to offer a heartfelt *thank you* to God and to His so-mighty and glorious angels!

WORKS CITED

Hughes, Merritt Y., Editor. *John Milton: Complete Poems and Major Prose.* Odyssey Press, 1980. See *Paradise Lost*, Book IX, lines 782-785.

Luibheid.

The VIRTUES

By the intercession *of St. Michael and the celestial choir of Virtues, may the Lord preserve us from evil and suffer us not to fall into temptation. Amen.*

The Virtues rank fifth among the nine angel choirs, and so they hold a central place in the celestial hierarchy, with four choirs above and four below.

We encounter the Virtues by name only once in Scripture: *Christ is above all principality and power and virtue and dominion.* *(Ephesians 1:21)*

Dionysius uses the name "Authorities" in place of "Virtues" when discussing this angel choir. For him:

the Authorities "are so placed that they can receive God in a harmonious and unconfused way . . . . Far from employing their authoritative powers to do tyrannous harm to the inferiors, they are harmoniously and unfailingly uplifted toward the things of God.   *(Luibheid, p. 167)*

The Chaplet's use of "Virtues" is a departure from Dionysius, and we will adhere to the Chaplet designation. It is well worth noting that, as used here, the concept of virility entails more than the narrow definition posited by the Latin root word, *vir*, meaning "man." Rather, it speaks also (regardless of gender) to the qualities of "moral excellence and righteousness; goodness …a particularly efficacious, good or beneficial quality." *(Berube, p. 1351)*

With the salutation to the Virtues, we ask for a pair of closely related gifts of heaven:

> May the Lord preserve us from evil and
> [the Lord] suffer us not to fall into temptation.

The wording here calls to mind immediately the closing lines of the Our Father, or the Lord's Prayer – at once so similar and so starkly different, that we are naturally inclined to compare and contrast the two prayers, namely, the Chaplet and the Lord's Prayer. And so we start with that most famously vexing line contained in the latter:

> *… lead us not into temptation.*
> *(cf. Matthew 6.13 and Luke 11.4)*

The conundrum lies in the discomfiting notion that God could or would lead us to sin. Foremost among many contemporary Church authorities to address the issue is Pope Francis. During a General Audience, the Holy Father explained that the present-day text is

> "not a good translation because it speaks of a God who induces temptation." He continues by making an important distinction: "I am the one who falls; it's not [God] who pushes me toward temptation to see how I fall. A father doesn't do this, a father helps us to get up right away." *(The Guardian)*

Pope Francis' remarks echo the teaching contained in the New Testament letter of James:

> *No one experiencing temptation should say, "I am being*
> *tempted by God, for God is not subject to temptation to*
> *evil and he himself tempts no one." (James 1.13)*

As if to underscore this key difference from any implication that the Lord might somehow lead or tempt us to sin and evil, the Chaplet prayer is one that the Lord may *preserve* us from evil. It is noteworthy here that the word "preserve," when used as a verb, or action word, as it is used in the Chaplet, denotes a *proactive* measure: (emphasis added)

1.) To keep (something) in its original state or in good condition,
2.) To keep (something) safe from harm or loss: TO PROTECT, and
3.) To prevent (food) from spoiling or going bad. www.merriam-webster.com

Incorporating these several definitions as we pray, our petition in the Chaplet equates essentially to *do not let us fall into evil **to begin with.*** (Emphasis mine) Rather, preserve us, free from sin and evil.

The Chaplet prayer that the Lord preserve us from evil leads to another comparison and contrast consideration of the Lord's Prayer:

CHAPLET: preserve us from evil
OUR FATHER: deliver us from evil

As noted previously, the word "preserve" signifies pro-action, while, on the other hand, the word "deliver" suggests an after-the-fall state of affairs. That is, we have already lapsed into evil and so pray that we may be delivered. The primary definition of "deliver," again, according to *Merriam-Webster* online, is to *set free.* The list of like words, or synonyms, accompanying the definition gives a beautifully nuanced sense of *redemption*:

Rescue/redeem/ransom/reclaim/save

While we earnestly hope and pray
"that [we] may not commit sin [that is, <u>preserve</u> us from

evil] *we know that if anyone does sin, we have an
Advocate with the Father, Jesus Christ, the righteous one.
He is expiation for our sins* [**deliver** us from evil].
(Emphasis mine)   *(cf. 1 John 2.1-2)*

God suffering?

In further meditation of this salutation to the Virtues, we focus on the second gift we ask from heaven, that is, *suffer us not to fall into temptation.*   Stop for a moment. Go back and reread the last line above slowly, and contemplate carefully the last three words: the Lord suffer… The Lord *suffering.* How is it possible that Christ, once slain, and now risen to everlasting glory at God's right hand, could possibly suffer? As St. Paul says, "we know that Christ, raised from the dead, dies no more, death no longer has power over him . . . he died once and for all" *(Romans 6. 9-10).* Yet, it is to this same Apostle to the Gentiles that we turn for some insight into the mystery of God suffering.

1. *The Conversion of St. Paul*
In the Acts of the Apostles, we encounter the irrepressible young rabbi Saul, bound for Damascus to seize *"any men and women who belonged to the Way [so that] he might bring them back to Jerusalem in chains." (Acts 9.2)* Such was his intent when he was instead blinded by a dazzling bright light from the sky. And out of this light, he heard a voice asking:

Saul, Saul, why are you persecuting **Me**?

In reply, Saul manages to ask, *"Who are you, sir?"* The unambiguous reply would thoroughly win over the heart of a zealous young man destined for the crown of martyrdom:

I AM Jesus, whom you are persecuting.

The correlation is unmistakable. Our Lord is so intimately united to his faithful ones that, even though He is enthroned in majesty, He nonetheless identifies with their suffering as if it were His own.

2. *The Mystical Body of Christ*

Again we turn to St. Paul for his teaching on one of the most sublime mysteries of our faith, that is, our shared unity as members of Christ's Mystical Body:

As a body is one though it has many parts, and all the parts of the body, though many, are one body, so also Christ: the body is not a single part, but many...if one part suffers, all the parts suffer with it. (1 Corinthians 12.12)

All the parts suffer, including . . . *"Christ [Who] is the head of the body, the church." (Colossians 1.18)*

From our communion with Christ *"in [Whom] we live and move and have our being," (Acts 17.28)* it follows that our good works and sinful deeds, far from affecting only us who perform them, can and do exert a beneficial or damaging effect on the *entire* body and *all* its members. What profound and shared responsibility do we have!

A final consideration of this blessed choir of Virtues follows from the very name of the choir itself, and with this, we return to the broader definition of *vir* and reflect that a life filled with courage, honor, strength may well be esteemed virtuous. But there remains a higher level, a "still more excellent way" (*1 Corinthians 12.31*) for all who aspire to an authentic Christ-centered life, and we find this in the Seven Cardinal ***Virtues***:

Prudence
Fortitude
Faith
Hope
Temperance
Justice
Charity – *"the greatest of [all]" (1 Corinthians 13.13)*

WORKS CITED

Berube

https://www.merriam-webster.com/preserve

https://www.theguardian.com.dec. Sherwood, Harriet and agency. December 8, 2017, 08.17 EST "Lead us not into mistranslation: pope wants Lord's Prayer changed." (*Luibheid*)

The Orthodox Cathedral of St. Mark, Alexandria, Egypt

The POWERS

By the intercession of St. Michael and the celestial choir of *Powers, may the Lord vouchsafe to protect our souls from the snares and temptations of the devil. Amen.*

The sixth angel choir is the mighty Powers, a name especially well-suited to these servants of our omnipotent God, entrusted by Him with the safeguarding of our precious, immortal souls.

Scripture references to the Powers are found in both Old and New Testaments. The Book of Daniel, relating the fiery furnace ordeal of God's faithful servants Shadrach, Meshach and Abednego, contains an exquisite hymn of praise to God, including the couplet:

> *All you **powers**, bless the Lord;*
> *Praise and exalt him above all forever.* (Emphasis added)
> *(Daniel 3.61)*

As we have seen in the New Testament, St. Paul mentions the Powers in his letters to the Ephesians and Colossians. Joining St. Paul in proclaiming the pre-eminence and sovereignty of Christ above all the angels is St. Peter, who writes:

> *Jesus Christ has gone into heaven and is at the right*
> *hand of God, with angels, authorities and powers subject*
> *to him.* *(1 Peter 3.22)*

According to Dionysius:
 . . . the title [of the Powers] refers to a kind of masculine and unshakable courage in all its godlike activities. It is a courage that abandons all laziness and softness during the

reception of the divine enlightenments granted to it., and is powerfully uplifted to imitate God. *(Luibheid, p. 167)*

Following are a half dozen definitions of the word *power* which together greatly expound its meaning and enrich our understanding of its various applications:

1. the ability or capacity to act or perform effectively,
2. a specific capacity, faculty or aptitude,
3. strength or force exerted; might,
4. the ability of official capacity to exercise control; authority,
5. forcefulness; effectiveness, and
6. *archaic:* an armed force

(Berube, pgs. 971-972)

With the salutation to the Powers, St. Michael inspires us to ask for the heavenly gift that the Lord may graciously protect our souls against the snares and temptations of the devil.

We are signally blessed that the Powers are associated with this great favor. Taking into account the aforementioned definitions of the word power, we may infer that the members of this celestial choir operate effectively in obedience to God's holy will. They wield a tremendous might and strength by means of their God-given authority. Together they comprise a cohesive, indomitable force specially armed and arrayed for spiritual warfare—under the leadership of the Prince of the Heavenly Host, St. Michael.

With these corollaries in mind, let us consider the gift we implore in the salutation to the Powers while also recalling the favor we sought by the intercession of the Virtues:

POWERS: may the Lord *protect our souls*
VIRTUES: may the Lord *preserve* us

The particular focus on "our souls" in the salutation to the Powers, compared to the all-encompassing "us" in the preceding prayer to the Virtues naturally leads us to reflect on the possible reason(s) for such specificity. Why should "our souls" be singled out apart from, in addition to, "us"? Why the emphasis? Perhaps Church teaching offers some insight for this important distinction, defining the soul as:

> the innermost aspect of man, that which is of greatest value in him, that by which he is most especially in God's image: "soul" signifies the spiritual principle in man. (*CCC 363*)

Our immortal soul, created to participate most intimately in relationship with God and all members of the human family, is the supremely prized quarry of the devil. And indeed, with a seething hatred for God and jealous contempt for man – made in the image and likeness of God – Satan is continually on the prowl. Like a rabid, crazed beast, he is driven, always seizing an opportunity to lunge madly at the most vital part of his prey. To continue the analogy, the beast looks instinctively to crush the windpipe and rip the jugular to ensure the death of its prey. (See notes). Efficiently. *Irreparably.* Just so, the Evil One strives to sunder and destroy our communion with God and one another. This is the crux of spiritual warfare.

Not surprisingly, perhaps, the holy Powers whose aid we implore for the especial protection of our immortal souls appear to be particularly involved in this most critical struggle. As renowned exorcist Monsignor Stephen J. Rosetti writes:

> We have been given to understand that, even now, St. Michael is spiritually present at every exorcism. Also, we understand that at least one, and maybe more, from the

Powers of heaven . . . are at the exorcist's side in the daily battle for the oppressed.[8]   *(Rosetti, p. 23)*

Rosetti again remarks:

> Of the nine choirs of angels, it is thought that the rank of Powers is particularly present in exorcisms. These angelic Powers are of a higher rank than that of the guardian angels and thus have greater power in assisting in the casting out of demons. *(Rosetti, p. 6)*

One final note on the Powers is suggested by the wording of the Prayer to St. Michael composed by Pope Leo XIII. The Holy Father fairly adjures the Warrior Archangel with particularly stirring lines:

> … and do thou, O Prince of the Heavenly Host, by the **Power** (emphasis added) of God, cast into hell Satan and all the evil spirits . . .

Rather conspicuous is the Pontiff's choice of words: it is by the **power** of God that St. Michael overcomes Satan and his legions. Not the might or the strength of God. Not His surpassing mercy or boundless wisdom. But by His **power**. Perhaps, even if unintentional, Pope Leo's invocation of the Power of God in his prayer of exorcism offers a subtle insight into, and recognition of, the angel choir entrusted with the safety and protection of our immortal souls.

---

[8] Monsignor Rosetti writes, "demons choke people [because] it is something animals do. They grab their prey by the throat to subdue and it and to kill it." *(Rosetti, p. 23)*

WORKS CITED

Berube

Catechism of the Catholic Church. Image, an imprint of Crown Publishing Corp, a Division of Random House, 1995

Luibheid

Rosetti, Monsignor Stephen J. *Diary of an American Exorcist: Demons, Possession and the Modern Day Battle Against Evil.* Sophia Institute Press. 2021.

THE PRINCIPALITIES

By the intercession *of St. Michael and the celestial choir of Principalities, may God fill our souls with a true spirit of obedience. Amen.*

Having reflected on the Powers with their special charge for the protection of souls, we encounter next the seventh angel choir, the Principalities who also have a special care for our souls. Scripture references to these angels are ones we have already noted in the writings of St. Paul; however, the Apostle's letter to the Ephesians includes a further mention:

To me [Paul] this grace was given, to preach to the Gentiles the inscrutable riches of Christ, and to bring to light [for all] what is the plan of the mystery hidden from ages past in God who created all things . . . so that the manifold wisdom of God might now be made known through the church to the principalities and authorities in heaven.   *(Ephesians 3.8-10)*

Concerning the Principalities, Dionysius writes:

The term "heavenly principalities" refers to those who possess a godlike and princely hegemony, with a sacred order most suited to princely powers ... *(Luibheid, p.170)*

I would like to propose a rather different interpretation of these angels, starting with their Choir name. As noted previously with the choir of Thrones, the Principalities are called by a name rich with lofty connotation and majestic ring. We think of heirs apparent; the royal progeny of kings. To such as these, subjects accord high honor and potentates make obeisance. Yet, we must stop and recall that the Principalities, like the Thrones and all the angel choirs of heaven, serve the God Who *"emptied himself, taking the form of a slave ... he humbled himself, becoming obedient unto death, even death on a cross."* (*Philippians* 2. 7-8) Just as this is no ordinary prince after human fashion, so it is no common gift we seek by the intercession of the Principalities:

May God fill our souls with a true spirit of obedience.

This single line reads so quickly and straightforwardly that our attention naturally settles on the final words, "true spirit of obedience." Yet, an exquisitely subtle and understated clue gives some sense of the singular preciousness of this gift, obedience. Do you see it? This is the only salutation with the words "May *God;*" all the others use "May *the Lord.*" **May God** . . . consider the uniqueness. Consider the immediacy, and perhaps also forcefulness and urgency, achieved when we omit the titular-sounding article *the.*

While the prayer addressed to the Principalities is unique among the Chaplet salutations, I believe it shares a rich complementarity with the prayer to the choir of Thrones. The two salutations work in tandem as an appeal to grow in imitation of Christ, our pre-eminent Model of humility and obedience. Following is a line-by-line comparison of the wording of the two salutations and the heavenly gifts we implore:

T(hrones)	may the Lord
P(rincipalities)	may God
T	infuse into our hearts
P	fill our souls
T	with a true and sincere spirit
P	with a true spirit
T	of humility
P	of obedience

Obedience. Hard, exacting proof of love: *"If you love Me, you will keep My words,"* (*John 14.15*) and *"greater love has no one than this, to lay down one's life for one's friends."* (*John 15.13*) The virtue seems so intractably and diametrically opposed to our fallen, rebellious human nature. But for the grace and gift of God, it can be so virtually unattainable. All the more so, we pray in blunt earnest, with an economy of words: *may God fill our souls ...*

It is often said that "pride goeth before a fall." There can be no more heinous demonstration of pride and the fall that invariably results, than the rebellion of the erstwhile Light-bearer angel of heaven, Lucifer. Flush with injured pride; stirred to flagrant rebellion against the Divine Will, Lucifer-become-Satan dared to assert equality with God. In the book of the Prophet Isaiah, we find words of the rulers of Babylon – words attributed also to the Evil One – a chilling manifesto of the pride that was Satan's downfall:

> *In your heart you said:*
> *'I will scale the heavens;*
> *Above the stars of God*
> *I will set up my throne;*
> *I will take my seat on the Mount of Assembly.*
> *On the heights of Zaphon*
> *I will ascend above the tops of the clouds:*
> ***I will be like the Most High!'*** *(*Emphasis added).
> *(Isaiah 14.13-14)*

Isaiah continues, narrating the consequences – the fall without compare:

> *No! Down to Sheol you will be brought*
> *To the depths of the pit! ...*
> *Going down to the very stones of the pit.*
> *(Isaiah 14.15,19)*

Perhaps, if in our broken world pride leads one to fall, so in the divine realm, humility disposes one to obedience. The Chaplet seems to aver as much – we pray first for the gift of humility, by the intercession of the Thrones, and after, for the favor of obedience by the intercession of the Principalities. Humility … obedience … eternal life:

> *For the sake of the joy that lay before him [Jesus] endured the cross, despising its shame, and has taken his seat at the right of the throne of God.*
>
> *(Hebrews 12.2)*

> *[For Jesus' becoming obedient unto death ... on a cross] . . . God greatly exalted Him and bestowed upon Him the name that is above every other name, so that at the Name of Jesus, every knee in the heavens, on the earth and under the earth must bend, and every tongue proclaim to the glory of God the Father:*

JESUS CHRIST IS LORD!
Philippians 2.9-11

WORKS CITED

Luibheid

Michaelskirche, Vienna, Austria

The ARCHANGELS

By the intercession of St. Michael and the celestial choir of Archangels, may the Lord give us perseverance in faith and in all good works, in order that we gain the glory of Paradise. Amen.

The eighth celestial choir is that of the Archangels, and it is to this small[9] and glorious company that the blessed Archangels Saints Michael, Gabriel and Raphael belong.

Both Old and New Testament Scriptures are rich with mention of the esteemed Archangel trio, from the book of Daniel and Tobit to the Gospel of Saint Luke and the Book of Revelation.[10]

Dionysius comments on the choir of Archangels as it is found below the choir of Principalities and above that of the Angels:

> The holy archangels have the same order as the heavenly principalities and … [The order of archangels] communes with the most holy principalities and with the holy angels … it brings about the unity of the angels. *(Luibheid, p. 170)*

With the salutation to the Archangels, we ask for the twofold heavenly gifts of

> perseverance in faith and
> [perseverance] in all good works

---

[9] In the Old Testament book of Tobit, the Archangel Raphael reveals that he is "one of the *seven* angels who stand and serve before the Glory of the Lord." *(Tobit 12:15)* (Emphasis mine)

[10] Michael: *Daniel 10, 12, Jude 1, Rev 12*; Gabriel: *Daniel 8, 9, Luke 1;* Raphael: *Tobit 12. See Appendix I.*

Interestingly, and unique to this salutation, our petition continues and culminates with a direct object of sorts as we read in the phrase:

in order that we gain the glory of Paradise.

Accordingly, we see in the wording of our prayer to the Archangels a definitive cause-and-effect relationship between faith and good works on one hand, and gaining the glory of Paradise on the other. The wording admits no ambiguity, no equivocation. Rather, it reminds us of the teaching of the Apostle St. James:

Be doers of the word and not hearers only. (James 1.22)

Be **doers** of the word – **live** the faith!

Lest we overlook the imperative at work here or perhaps fail to appreciate the gravitas, the Apostle bluntly cautions:

Faith without works is dead. (cf. James 2.17)

The Chaplet thus affirms the unbroken apostolic teaching and tradition of the Church. At the same time, it invites us to contemplate the threefold choice gifts associated with the Archangels, namely, perseverance, faith, and all good works.

PERSEVERANCE

Perseverance is a theme of heroic import throughout Scripture. Time after time, whether in Abraham's insistent prayer for the virtuous inhabitants of Sodom and Gomorrah, the patient endurance of the long-suffering Job or the resilience of the Early Church in the face of persecution, we see epitomized such qualities as fidelity, steadfastness; constancy. All derive from a certain visceral determination to hold fast to the faith and stay the course even unto death. St. Paul's second letter to Timothy offers a summation that, for the Apostle's pending martyrdom, is all the more poignant:

> *I have fought the good fight.*
> *I have finished the course.*
> *I have kept the faith. (2 Timothy 4.7)*

These are the words of a champion who has proven himself faithful to a Christ-centered life, despite all the myriad trials, adversities and stumbling blocks he encountered. By grace has he triumphed and now, of a certainty, the glory of Paradise awaits:

> *From now on a merited crown awaits me; on that day the Lord, just judge that He is, will award it to me and not only to me but to all who have looked for His appearing with eager longing born of faith. (2 Timothy 2.6-8)*

FAITH: I BELIEVE

STOP. Do not, *do not,* let yourself race absentmindedly past these opening words of the Creed. Take time instead to dwell on this precious word couplet. Do you perceive the peerless gift they are? Can you grasp the profound blessing it is to *own* these words and pray them from the heart? Consider how many countless individuals today have nothing or no one in which or in whom to believe. How many have steeled themselves against believing *anything*? Or who once believed but no longer? Are they not like the:

> *... person who built his house on sand [?] The rain came down, the streams rose and the winds blew and beat against that house, and it fell with a great crash [?] (Matthew 7.26-27)*

The specter of trying to navigate our world today, reeling as it is from war, tyranny, plague, terrorism, natural disaster, and so many more co-occurring ravages – without the gift of faith – is beyond terrifying:

> *. . . nations will be in anguish and perplexity at the roaring and tossing of the sea. People will faint from terror, apprehensive of what is coming on the world . . .*
> *(Luke 21.25-26)*

Yet, we are called to believe that the grace and mercy of God, Who made heaven and earth, will see us safely through. We are called to *trust* in Divine Mercy. (Emphasis added)

GOOD WORKS

FULL STOP. Savor the sound and definitiveness of this declaration. Although few and seemingly simple, the four words of this introductory statement of the Creed are both catalyst and charter for our lives. Among the countless ways this seminal expression of belief invites our careful, unhurried reflection is a syllogism:

I believe in God, therefore, I _______________.

We are challenged with a marvelous, bracing robustness: How does this faith make a difference in our lives? In what ways do we choose from moment to moment to fill in the blank? How do we (hopefully) allow these words to take root, shape and inform our lives? The possibilities are endless and we do well to ask for the aid of the holy angels. Let us live and act in such a way, persevering to the end of our days, until at last when all is said and done, we may hear the most blessed, affirming welcome of Our Lord Jesus:

*Come, ye blessed of my Father. Inherit the kingdom
prepared for you from the foundation of the world.
For I was hungry and you gave me to eat,
thirsty and you gave me to drink,
a stranger, and you welcomed me,
naked and you clothed me,
ill and you cared for me;
in prison and you visited me.*   (Matthew 25.34-36)

AMEN!

The ANGELS

By the intercession of St. Michael and the celestial choir of Angels, may the Lord grant us to be protected by them in this mortal life and conducted hereafter to eternal glory. Amen.

The last Chaplet salutation brings us to the ninth celestial choir of the Angels. Lowliest among the ranks of the Heavenly Hosts and farthest from the Throne of God, they dwell closest to us whom God was pleased to create *"little less than the angels"* (Cf. *Psalm 8.5*), that is, little less than they.

The Scriptures of both Testaments are replete with references to the angels. From Genesis to Revelation, these ethereal beings rarely seem far from the narrative of Salvation History. As divine messengers, theirs is a continual, albeit usually discrete, abiding presence among God's people, and they accomplish everything in perfect submission to the Divine Will.

According to Dionysius:

> ... the angels complete the entire ranking of the heavenly intelligences. Among the heavenly beings, it is they who possess the final quality of being an angel. For being closer to us, they, more appropriately than the previous ones, are named "angels" insofar as their hierarchy is more concerned with revelation and is closer to the world. (*Luibheid, p. 170*)

The two heavenly gifts we implore by the intercession of the angels are introduced with an elegant balance of sound and meter, which underscores their preciousness:

> To be protected . . . in this mortal life, and
> [to be] conducted . . . to eternal glory.

This salutation is distinctly noteworthy, as the angels are the only choir interceding in reference to themselves – even if only indirectly; using passive voice. This seems a decidedly odd thing for an angel to do. Nonetheless, based on their prayer, it seems that the angels genuinely *want* to be in our company – now and for all eternity. Their love of God and love of humanity animate them with an eagerness to share our journey. One thinks of the bounding enthusiasm of Isaiah as God weighs the choice of his emissary to Israel:

> *Here I am ... Send **me**!* (Emphasis added)
> *(Isaiah 6.8)*

Our prayer and that of the angels are mirror reflections of a shared and intimate longing. As much as we want to be protected, so they long to protect; and to be conducted, so they to conduct. Now and forever. Trusted with a ministry that encompasses eternity, these holy angels who *"always look upon the face of God in heaven, (Matthew 18.10)* want to be with us who are made in the image and likeness of God. For their particular office, these lowliest of angels constantly delight in the Beatific Vision. How wonderfully are they blessed – and we along with them!

A time-honored saying encourages people with the reminder that "more things are wrought by prayer than this world dreams of." Have you ever stopped and wondered just *how* exactly this prodigy of "things" might be accomplished? What agency could be at work? Perhaps we are really acknowledging the deeds and interventions of a sweet angel when we are moved to say:

> There but for the grace of God, I would have
> stepped into rush-hour traffic,
> missed a job interview, or
> failed my chemistry final.

Or again –

> Only by the grace of God did I
> balance my checking account,
> spot the right freeway exit in time, or
> reconcile with a long-lost sibling.

Might "grace" be an angel?[11]

WORKS CITED

Dods

Luibheid

---

[11] St. Augustine writes, ". . . we cannot but believe that all miracles . . . worked by angels . . . are worked by those who love us in a true and godly sort, through their means, God Himself working in them."   *(Dods, p. 284)*

PART III

COMPREHENSIVE WORKS CITED

Barbet, Pierre, M.D., *A Doctor at Calvary: The Passion of Our Lord Jesus Christ as Described by a Surgeon*. Trans. by the Earl of Wicklow. Image Books, A Division of Doubleday, 1963.

Berube, Margery S., Director of Editorial Operations. *The American Heritage Dictionary: Second College Edition*. Houghton Mifflin, 1982.

Bokenkotter, Thomas, *A Concise History of the Catholic Church*. Revised Edition, Image Books, Doubleday, 2005.

Catechism of the Catholic Church. First Ed., Image Books, 1995.

Dods, Marcus, D.D., translator, *The City of God*. By Saint Augustine of Hippo. Hendrickson Publishers, 2009.

Hardon, Rev. John A., S.J., *Modern Catholic Dictionary*. Eternal Life, 2008.

Hughes, Merritt Y., Editor, *John Milton: Complete Poems and Major Prose*. Odyssey Press, 1980. *Paradise Lost*, Book IX, lines 782-785.

Kalvelage, Brother Francis Mary, F.I., Editor, *Padre Pio: The Wonder Worker*. Franciscan Friars of the Immaculate, 2009.

Luibheid, Colm, translator, *Pseudo-Dionysius: The Complete Works*. Paulist Press, 1987.

Matthews, Rupert. *The Popes: Every Question Answered*. Thunder Bay Press, 2019.

Perkins, David, Editor. *English Romantic Writers*. Harcourt, Brace, Jovanovich, 1967: *Intimations of Immortality from*

Recollections of Early Childhood by William Wordsworth, V, line 65.

Pronechen, Joseph. "*The Powerful Chaplet Given by the Prince of Angels.*" *National Catholic Register*, 9-29, 2019.

Puschaver, Carol. Publication review for *Though War be Waged Upon Me: A Saint Michael Treasury of Prayer and Reflection* in **Plot, Line and Sinker**, a blog by Ellen Gable Hrkach, July 9, 2020.

Puschaver, Carol. *Though War Be Waged Upon Me: A Treasury of Saint Michael Treasury of Prayer and Reflection*. Self-published, 2019.

Rosetti, Msgr. Stephen J. *Diary of an American Exorcist.* Sophia Institute Press, 2021.

Simpson, D. P., *Cassell's New Latin Dictionary: Latin/English: English/Latin.* Funk and Wagnalls, 1962.

Thigpen, Paul. *Manual for Spiritual Warfare*. TAN, 2014.

https://www.merriam-webster.com/preserve

https://www.theguardian.com.dec.   Sherwood, Harriet and agency.   December 8, 2017, 08.17 EST "Lead us not into mistranslation: pope wants Lord's Prayer changed."

WORKS CONSULTED

Francis, Fr. Thomas, O.C.S.O. *Angels: From Body-Guards to Spirit-Directors*. Martino-White Printing, 1900.

Brown, Raymond E., S.S., et al, Editors. *The New Jerome Biblical Commentary*. Prentice Hall, 1990.

APPENDIX I
Scripture References to the Archangels:

MICHAEL, Who-is-Like-to God
The Warrior Archangel

Do not fear, Daniel . . . from the first day you made up your mind to acquire understanding and humble yourself before God, your prayer was heard. Because of it I started out, but the prince of the kingdom of Persian stood in my way for twenty-one days, until finally Michael, one of the chief princes, came to help me.   (Daniel 10:12-13)*

Soon I must fight the prince of Persia again... No one supports me against these except Michael, your prince ... **   *(Daniel 10.2)*

At that time there shall arise Michael, the great prince, guardian of your people; It shall be a time unsurpassed in distress since the nation began until that time. . .But those with insight shall shine brightly like the splendor of the firmament, and those who lead the many to justice shall be like the stars forever.   (Daniel 12.1,3)

. . . the archangel Michael, when he argued with the devil in a dispute over the body of Moses, did not venture to pronounce a reviling judgment upon him, but said, "May the Lord rebuke you!"   (Jude 1.9)

. . . war broke out in heaven; Michael and his angels battled against the dragon. The Dragon and its angels fought back, but they did not prevail. (Revelation 12.7)

*/**The speaker here is thought to be the Archangel Gabriel.

GABRIEL, Man of God
The Messenger Archangel

While I, Daniel, sought the meaning of the vision I had seen, one who looked like a man stood before me, and . . . I heard a human voice that cried out, "Gabriel, explain the vision to this man." When he came near where I was standing, I fell prostrate in terror. But he said to me, "Understand, O son of man, that the vision refers to the end of time." (Daniel 8.15-17)

. . . I was still praying, when the man, Gabriel, whom I had seen in vision before, came to me in flight at the time of the evening offering. He instructed me in these words, "Daniel, I have now come to give you understanding."
(Daniel 9.21-22)

Once when [Zechariah] was serving as priest in his division's turn before God . . . he was chosen by lot to enter the sanctuary of the Lord to burn incense. Then, when the whole assembly of the people was praying outside . . . the angel of the Lord appeared to him, standing at the right of the altar of incense. . . . "Do not be afraid, Zechariah . . . your wife Elizabeth will bear you a son, and you shall name him John . . . . Then Zechariah said to the angel, "How shall I know this? For I am an old man, and my wife is advanced in years." And the angel said to him in reply, "I am Gabriel, who stand before God. I was sent to speak to you and announce to you this good news." (Luke 1.8-13, 18-19)

The angel Gabriel was sent from God to a town of Galilee called Nazareth, to a virgin betrothed to a man named Joseph, of the house of David, and the virgin's name was Mary. And coming to her, he said, "Hail, favored one! The Lord is with you." But she was greatly troubled at what was said and pondered what sort of greeting this might be. Then the angel said to her, 'Do not be afraid, Mary, for you have found favor with God. Behold, you will conceive in your womb and bear a Son, and you shall name him Jesus.' (*Luke 1.26-31*)

RAPHAEL, God heals
The Healer Archangel

The Old Testament book of Tobit contains an angelophany quite remarkable in terms of its comprehensive scope and detail as it related the Archangel Raphael's interaction with the elderly Tobi and his son Tobias, both devout Israelites of the tribe of Napthali. Sent by God to heal father and son of physical, emotional, and spiritual afflictions, the Archangel takes the form of a young man with the name Azariah, meaning "'YHWH has helped:'"

Raphael called the two of them (Tobit and Tobias) aside privately and said to them: *'Bless God and give him thanks before all the living for the good things he has done for you. I shall now tell you the whole truth and conceal nothing at all from you. I have already said to you, 'A king's secret should be kept secret, but one must declare the works of God with due honor. . . . **I am Raphael, one of the seven angels who stand and serve before the Glory of the Lord.'*** (Emphasis added) *(Tobit 12.6,7,15)*

'. . . when I was with you, I was not acting out of any favor on my part, but by God's will. So bless God every day; give praise with song. Even though you saw me eat and drink, I did not eat or drink anything; what you were seeing was a vision. So now bless the Lord on earth and give thanks to God. Look, I am ascending to the One who sent me.' (*Tobit 12.6,11,15,18-20*)

WORK CITED

Luibheid

APPENDIX II

THE APOSTLES' CREED

I believe in God, the Father Almighty,
Maker of Heaven and earth,
and in Jesus Christ, His only Son Our Lord,
Who was conceived by the Holy Spirit,
born of the Virgin Mary,
suffered under Pontius Pilate, was crucified,
died and was buried.
He descended into Hell;
the third day He rose again from the dead;
He ascended into Heaven,
and sits at the right hand of God, the Father
Almighty; from whence He shall come to judge
the living and the dead.
I believe in the Holy Spirit, the holy Catholic Church,
the communion of saints, the forgiveness of sins,
the resurrection of the body and life everlasting. Amen.

(Public Domain)

PRAYING THE SAINT MICHAEL CHAPLET, WITH DIAGRAM

As previously noted, the St. Michael Chaplet may be said to consist of five parts:

> Introductory prayers,
> the Nine Salutations,
> the Four Our Fathers,
> Invocation prayer to St. Michael, and
> Closing prayers.

For those familiar with Our Lady's Rosary and its 5 decades, each with 10 Hail Marys beads, perhaps the most striking difference of the St. Michael Chaplet is its 9 triads, each with 3 Hail Mary beads. Another readily apparent difference is a St. Michael medal in the place usually reserved for the Crucifix.

After the Introductory prayers are the 9 triads which of course correspond to one of the nine celestial choirs of angels. The whole is arranged according to the Dionysian hierarchy, with the Seraphim as the highest, and the Angels as the lowest. Each triad starts with a salutary prayer addressed to both St. Michael and one of the specific angel choirs. The salutation is followed by one Our Father and three Hail Marys. In addition to the 9 triads is a section of four beads placed between a triad section and the St. Michael medal. One Our Father is recited on each of the four beads – one each in honor of the three Archangels named in Scripture: Saints Michael, Gabriel and Raphael, and finally one in honor of the Guardian Angel of the person praying the Chaplet.

The Chaplet then proceeds with the Invocation to St. Michael and Closing prayers.

THE SAINT MICHAEL CHAPLET

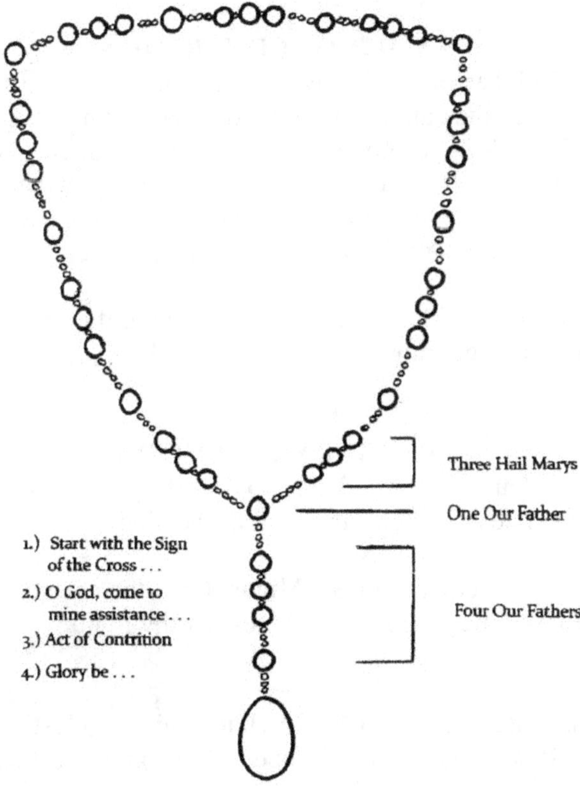

THE SAINT MICHAEL CHAPLET

+In the Name of the Father, and the Son and the Holy Spirit. Amen.

O God, come to mine assistance. Lord, make haste to help me.

AN ACT OF CONTRITION

Oh my God, I am sorry for my sins with all my heart. In choosing to do wrong, and failing to do good, I have sinned against You Whom I should love above all things. I firmly intend, with Your help, to make amends, to sin no more and to avoid whatever might cause me to sin. Our Lord and Savior Jesus Christ suffered and died for my sins. In His Name, my God, have mercy. Amen.

Glory be to the Father, and to the Son, and to the Holy Ghost, as it was in the beginning, is now, and ever shall be, world without end. Amen.

THE NINE SALUTATIONS

(Pray one Our Father and three Hail Marys after each of the following nine salutations in honor of the nine Choirs of Angels).

1. **By the intercession of St. Michael** and the celestial Choir of **SERAPHIM** may the Lord make us worthy to burn with the fire of perfect charity. Amen.

2. **By the intercession of St. Michael** and the celestial Choir of **CHERUBIM** may the Lord vouchsafe to grant us the grace to leave the ways of sin to run in the paths of Christian perfection. Amen.

3. **By the intercession of St. Michael** and the celestial Choir of **THRONES** may the Lord infuse into our hearts a true and sincere spirit of humility. Amen.

4. **By the intercession of St. Michael** and the celestial Choir of **DOMINIONS** may the Lord give us grace to govern our senses and subdue our unruly passions. Amen.

5. **By the intercession of St. Michael** and the celestial Choir of **VIRTUES** may the Lord preserve us from evil and suffer us not to fall into temptation. Amen.

6. **By the intercession of St. Michael** and the celestial Choir of **POWERS** may the Lord protect our souls against the snares and temptations of the devil. Amen.

7. **By the intercession of St. Michael** and the celestial Choir of **PRINCIPALITIES** may God fill our souls with a true spirit of obedience. Amen.

8. **By the intercession of St. Michael** and the celestial Choir of **ARCHANGELS** may the Lord give us perseverance in faith and in all good works in order that we gain the glory of Paradise. Amen.

9. **By the intercession of St. Michael** and the celestial Choir of **ANGELS** may the Lord grant us to be protected by them in this mortal life and conducted hereafter to eternal glory. Amen.

THE FOUR OUR FATHERS

Pray one Our Father in honor of each of the Archangels: Saint Michael, Saint Gabriel, Saint Raphael and also your Guardian Angel.

AN INVOCATION PRAYER TO ST. MICHAEL

O glorious prince St. Michael, chief and commander of the Heavenly Host, guardian of souls, vanquisher of rebel spirits, servant in the house of the Divine King and our most admirable conductor, you who shine with excellence and superhuman virtue, vouchsafe to deliver us from all evil, who turn to you with confidence and enable us by your gracious protection to serve God more and more faithfully every day. Amen.

V.) Pray for us, O glorious St. Michael, Prince of the Church of Jesus Christ,

R.) That we may be made worthy of His promises.

CLOSING CHAPLET PRAYER

Almighty and Everlasting God, Who, by a prodigy of goodness and a merciful desire for the salvation of all people, have appointed the most glorious Archangel St. Michael as Prince of Your Church, make us worthy, we implore You, to be delivered by his powerful protection from all our enemies, that none of them may harass us, especially at the hour of our death, but that we may be conducted by him into the august majesty of Your Divine Presence. This we beg through the infinite merits of Jesus Christ Our Lord. Amen.

END

ACKNOWLEDGMENTS

My heartfelt thanks to all who made this book possible:

Patty Sinay for creating a beautiful and captivating cover design.

Award-winning author Ellen Gable Hrkach and her husband James Hrkach for their inimitable printing, publishing, and artistic expertise.

Anne Costa, Elona (Puschaver) Gortz, Doctor Janet E. Jaffe and Kathy Kreinheder – four uniquely and remarkably talented women who together brought a wealth of diverse experience, background and perspective to bear on reading the manuscript. Their generous gifts of time and careful attention to detail have proven invaluable.

Pam Speach, owner of the Catholic Shop in Syracuse for her tireless encouragement and gracious hospitality in giving me quiet space and coffee and chocolate when I really needed a place to collect my thoughts and tease out a few paragraphs.

Rev. Darr Schoenhofen, who reviewed the manuscript and granted the *Nihil Obstat*.

All the prayer warriors near and far whose prayers saw me through dry spells when the words would just *not* come.

My sweetheart Guardian Angel who gave spiritual lights to me from time to time.

Saint Michael the Archangel, just because . . .

ABOUT THE AUTHOR

Carol Puschaver earned her Bachelor's and Master's degrees in English from Kent State University, Ohio, and lives in Upstate New York. She is a lifelong scholar, amateur historian, and world traveler who has taught courses on the Great Medieval Cathedrals of Europe and the Norman Conquest of England. As if born to ask *what, how* and *why* seemingly about *everything* (much to the perennial vexation of her family) she has an irrepressible curiosity as well as a lively sense of adventure and playfulness. Most of all, she is especially devoted to the Sacred Heart of Jesus in the Most Blessed Sacrament and to Saint Michael the Archangel.

Canterbury Cathedral, England

Also by Carol Puschaver
Though War Be Waged Upon Me:
A Saint Michael Treasury of Prayer and Reflection.

ST. MICHAEL the ARCHANGEL, defend
us in battle! Be our defense against the
wickedness and snares of the devil. May
God rebuke him, we humbly pray, and do
thou, O Prince of the Heavenly Host, by the
power of God, cast into hell Satan and all
the evil spirits who prowl around the world
seeking the ruin of souls. Amen.

Pope Leo XIII